DATE DUE

GRAMERCY GREAT MASTERS

Paul Klee

Gramercy Books
New York • Avenel

Acknowledgments

The publishers would like to thank the museums for reproduction permission and in particular the **BRIDGEMAN ART LIBRARY** for their help in supplying the illustrations for the book.

Christie's, London: Miniature; City of Churches; The Fish in the Harbor; Still Life with Thistle; Mural from the Temple of Yearning Thither; The Castle; Stage Rehearsal; View of G; Untitled; Mystic Ceramic; Around the Kernel; Still Life with Casket; Cathedral.
Galerie Slang, Munich: Growth of Nocturnal Plants.
Galerie Rosengart, Lucerne: Flowers in Stone.
Kunstmuseum, Basel: Motif from Hammamet; Senecio.
Kunstmuseum, Hanover: Flower Myth; Rotation.
Kunsthalle, Hamburg: The Gold Fish.
Kunstmuseum, Bern: Park near Lu(cerne); Insula Dulcamara.
Mayor Gallery, London: Garden; Ad Parnassum.
Museo Ca Pesaro, Venice: Still Life with Snake.
Private Collections: Fugue in Red; Flotilla; Sun and Moon; Dwarf (Fairy Tale).
Sammlung Felix Klee, Bern: Sentimental Virgin with Daisy; Garden Scene with Watering Cans; Bastard.
Stadtische Galerie in Lenbachhaus, Munich: Garden Still Life with a Watering Can; South Wind in Marc's Garden.
Stadelsches Kunstinstitut, Frankfurt: The Lamb.
Tate Gallery, London: Young Girl's Adventure.

Published by Gramercy Books
a division of Random House Value Publishing, Inc.
40 Engelhard Avenue
Avenel, New Jersey 07001

Printed and bound in Italy

ISBN 0-517-18221-1

10 9 8 7 6 5 4 3 2

Paul Klee
His Life and Works

Paul Klee has always been an enigma, equally at home with the abstract and the absolute, the emotion and the intellect. A painter of many styles and techniques, he was also a philosopher and a poet, a man who read Greek poetry in the original and who, resourceful and pragmatic, used his Munich kitchen as a studio so he could look after his young son and cook the family meals. Klee was also a talented violinist and it was not until he was a young adult that he decided to devote himself to art.

Paul Klee, the artist, was a member of the legendary Bauhaus, the international school and philosophy that aimed to combine art and craft into a functional lifestyle, to ultimately create a kind of "gothic cathedral" where artists and artisans could make a master structure that was both beautiful and functional.

Klee 's admirers would visit him in Germany and, later, after his work was considered "degenerate" by the Nazis and he was forced to flee, in Bern, Switzerland. Except for that Munich kitchen, Klee's studios were clean and orderly, as was he.

Paul Klee was a calm man who, more than any other artist, seemed to find the inner and outer balance in his vision. He spoke little. He didn't have to explain himself—his work, the ultimate self-expression, spoke for him. His small, self-contained paintings were his voice, perhaps the first "multi-media" creations. The paintings needed their titles to be completely defined—and each title needed a painting to become a whole greater than the sum of its parts.

He was inspired as much by primitivism, by childhood drawings, by the walls of Pompeii and the hot, vibrant colors of Africa as he was by the fish he saw in a Naples aquarium. He used hiero-glyphic-like symbols to create his own language, a combination of deceptively simple compositions with lines that almost speak from the canvas with witty and ironic words. His work was emotional and analytical, logical and fantastical, individual and cosmic.

Klee worked with both his right and left hands, equally com-fortable with either, although he preferred using his left hand for drawing and his right for writing.

When Klee died he left almost nine thousand pieces of art as well as the publications and the diaries he wrote from 1897 to 1918—an important source for his poetic theories, his painting, and his inspiration. In short, he left behind a rich legacy that despite all the information it imparts is perhaps like a Klee paint-ing: full of contradiction, an enigma like the man—both clear and ambiguous at the same time.

THE EARLY FACE OF PAUL KLEE

Paul Klee was born on December 18, 1879, in the town of Munchenbouchsee outside Bern, Switzerland. Hans Klee, his German father, was a trained singer but had failed to achieve the fame he envisioned. Instead, circumstances forced him to become a teacher in Bern. His disappointment was the source of sarcasm that, more often than not, was directed at his son. Perhaps it was his desire to please his father that made young Klee, already trained in the violin, consider becoming a singer. Klee inherited his father's sharp wit, but it was softer, an ironic humor that was evident in his later paintings, in his interplay between images, symbols, and words.

Klee's mother, Ida Maria Frick, was from Basle, a city consid-ered the most expressive, sensual, and sophisticated in Switzerland. She, too, studied to become a singer, at the Stuttgart Conservatory, but she met the charming, witty Hans and never began a professional career. She was sensitive, devoted to her son, and continued to encourage his artistic bent. Ida became partially paralyzed in 1906 and her illness brought them even closer. On the day she died in 1921 Klee dreamed of a woman, a ghost, float-ing through his studio. Perhaps the stark black borders on such paintings as *The Gate of Night*, which date from this time, relate to the grief he felt at his mother's death.

When Klee was seven, he began studying the violin. At eleven he performed with the Bern municipal orchestra but later gave it up for painting. But it was a soulful decision, one that he meditated upon in his voluminous diary entries. He wrote, "For me, music is like a woman bewitched by love"; and indecisively, "Will painting bring me glory? I could become a writer . . . " But ultimately he turned to art because he felt that his painting "lagged behind and needed to be given attention." But music was never far from his heart. His great passion for Mozart, for the sounds and composition of music, can be seen in the lines, the construction, and even some of the symbols in his many paintings.

Klee's childhood and adolescence were stable. Not only were his parents devoted to him, but so, too, was his maternal grandmother. When he was four, she gave him a box of colored chalk. She read him fairy tales that inspired his childhood drawings and showed him prints of the religious subjects that she held dear.

Another major influence in Klee's early life was his uncle, a restaurateur who lived in the countryside outside Bern, in Beatenberg. Klee loved the marble tops of the tables in his uncle's restaurant. He saw grotesque monsters and fascinating shapes in the marble's swirls and texture, and he copied these with a pencil.

Other childhood influences also shaped the future artist. There were, for instance, the Christmas trees, those mystical symbols of happiness and bittersweet memories that were to have a significant affect on his art. These trees evolved into the pine trees found in much of Klee's work, especially those he painted with the vivid colors he "brought back" from his 1914 trip to Tunisia.

And then there were the cats. Bern was famous for the multitude of cats that roamed through the city. Klee loved these cats, and like Picasso and his owls, many of his paintings feature a cat in a corner or on a floating table as a pictorial essence of sensuality. Klee was so devoted to his pet cat, Bimbo, that later when he was away teaching he would often write his wife asking only about Bimbo.

Klee had one sibling, a sister named Mathilde who was neither artistic nor musical. Nevertheless, they were close and she was devoted to him throughout her life and supported him in all his endeavors. Klee's love for her and their bond is evident in his penetrating, well-known portrait *The Artist's Sister* (1903).

Klee's education was complete and thorough. He went to

elementary school in 1886, followed by preparatory school and the Literarschule, where he continued to study Greek and Latin. He didn't particularly care for academic subjects, although he did fairly well. The only subject that he felt any passion for was Greek, and he continued to read Greek poetry in the original until his death. Throughout those early years he played his violin and he drew—ten sketchbooks from these early years survive.

After he graduated from school in 1898 Klee called himself a "future painter." The decision was made. He was nineteen years old.

THE STRUGGLING ARTIST

Klee, like other young artists at the turn of the century, had a choice. He could go to Paris or to Munich. Both capitals were cultural centers to which aspiring, as well as established, artists were drawn.

Perhaps because of his Germanic roots, Klee chose Munich. When he first arrived in October 1898, Klee was refused admission to the Academy, the most prestigious art school in the city. The admissions adviser suggested that he attend Heinrich Knirr's private drawing school to improve his figure drawing.

His life was full: he took his drawing lessons, went to the opera and the theater, and, of course, went out with young women. He wrote, "We often skipped school. First of all, I had to become a man. Art would follow from that."

Music was still a great passion. He would often spend peaceful musical evenings in the homes of cultured, middle-class families. On one of these evenings, he met Lily Stumpf, a pianist, at her parents' home. Klee was very much attracted to Lily and wanted her to be his wife but they would not marry for eight years (the time he felt he needed to achieve artistic maturity). She calmed him and helped him to focus his imagination.

By 1900 Klee had gained enough experience to attend Franz von Stuck's painting courses at the Academy. He learned a great deal from von Stuck, but it frustrated him that his use of color was still inadequate, although he achieved some mastery of watercolor techniques and of drawing.

But these three years were hardly a waste. Klee began to gain confidence in himself. He analyzed everything he did, everything

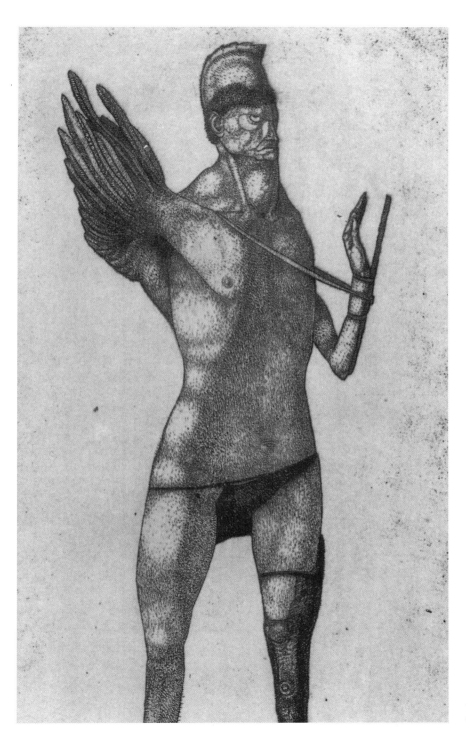

*Hero with
One Wing* (detail)

he thought, a process that would become part of his painting style. His rigorous self-discipline was extraordinary—and extremely organized. He once wrote down all the names of the young women he had met and wanted to sleep with. The last name on this long list was Lily. Next to her name he wrote: "Wait."

More than anything else, these years in Munich were a period of frustration—waiting for Lily, for art. Even von Stuck was irritating. He was not particularly impressed with Klee and he suggested the young artist take a course in sculpture. Instead, Klee became more determined than ever to paint. Although he wrote to his parents that "without question painting is the most difficult of all the arts," he knew that it would be the one medium that would allow him to express his personality completely. Before leaving Munich to return to Bern in the summer of 1901, he wrote: "I shall make painting take steps forward."

And he did just that.

To Italy

Many of Klee's friends went to Paris after Munich. But Klee felt he was not yet ready for Paris. He wanted to be more sure of himself and what he wanted to accomplish with his art. To that end, in the autumn of 1901, he went to Italy with his friend and fellow Academy student, the sculptor Hermann Haller. It was a classic tour of the country, one made by many middle-class students after they'd completed their studies. The difference lay in Klee himself—and in the influence of Italy on his work. He spent seven months in Italy. First he visited Milan, where he was impressed with the contrasts of light and dark used by the Renaissance painter Tintoretto. But he was not impressed by the art of the other Renaissance painters he saw in his visits to Florence, Rome, and Naples. Although Rome appealed to his senses and he delighted in the stimulation—the drinking, the joy, the life of the city— he was not as impressed with the ancient masters. The Sistine Chapel bewildered him and Michelangelo's *Pieta* left him cold. The Byzantine mosaics of San Giovanni, however, astounded him. The primitive quality of some of the early Gothic sculptures excited him, and the frescoes of Pompeii made him feel they were "painted and discovered" just for him.

Klee allowed his feelings to simmer, to mature, before he

14

Girl with Jugs
(detail)

expressed them in his art. The fish, the shells, the octopus in the inky waters of the Naples aquarium, the boats he saw in the waters of Genoa, the Christmas trees that so affected him as a child—all these would later make an appearance, in such paintings as *The Tree House*, *Fish Magic*, *Fish in the Port*, *The Gold Fish*, *Mystic Ceramic*. The more he saw in Italy, the more his ideas, his gentle irony, his satire, took hold.

Klee returned to Bern sporting a beard and wishing to honor the men of ancient times. He was ready to take hold of his art, to claim it—and life—for his own.

MASTERING FATE

Although Klee was developing his art quickly, it was all in his journal. It was not yet a visual reality.

He settled into a routine of sorts. He wrote, he read. He earned money by giving drawing lessons and playing the violin with the Bern municipal orchestra. He visited Lily in Munich, which also gave him a chance to see other art. It was in Munich that he saw William Blake's visionary drawings, which he admired. He was also astonished by Goya; he considered his drawings ideals he would never achieve.

In 1903 Klee began a series of fifteen engravings on zinc plate called *Inventions* and *Opus I*. One of these etchings, *Hero with One Wing* was among the first pieces Klee sold—for three hundred marks. It has the symbolic feel, the flow of erotic line, of Blake. Klee's comment about it was evidence of his wry sense of humor: it was inspired by the Wright Brothers' attempt to fly. In 1906, in Munich, Klee had his first exhibition, which was comprised of these etchings. The critics were not impressed. One wrote: "It is very difficult to give any sort of clear picture of the crazy anatomy of these forms."

But that was still a year in the future. In June 1905, Klee had not yet exhibited; he was still working on his etchings. He took a two-week trip to Paris where, although he saw the work of the Impressionists, he avoided contact with the young Parisian artists. Ironically, it was the Leonardo da Vinci work in the Louvre that he admired and that rekindled the admiration he'd first felt on his trip to Italy.

After his trip he began a series of twenty-five paintings "behind

16

glass." These paintings were more natural than his etchings. A few of them, such as *Garden Scene with a Watering Can*, even have an Impressionistic feel. Glass painting became a passion for Klee and over the next twelve years he returned to it again and again.

Painting on glass has a long tradition in Bavaria, but Klee's glass paintings reflect exhaustive research, analysis, and study, as well as sly humor. In the past, black had been painted on white glass. Klee reversed the process by covering the glass with black paint and then using a needle to etch his image in white.

For Klee the process was as important as the image. He combined different materials—glass or metal, burlap, newspaper, or plain white paper—through various techniques. *Portrait of My Father* and *Little Girl with Doll* (1905), for example, fuse etching and painting. These glass paintings do not have the vital color that mark Klee's mature work but they do signal the transition from the graphic design of his drawings and etchings to his fully realized paintings.

Although Klee worked diligently, he felt very much alone in Bern. There were few artists around him; he felt stifled and unstimulated. His friends were his music and his literature. During this period he studied anatomy with Professor Strasser. Although he found the precision of anatomy boring in Munich, he became engrossed by it in Bern. He began to draw nudes in carefully contrived situations that frequently helped to solve something Klee had been thinking about. *Female Nude Having Drunk, Pouring Out and Spitting as an Expression of Disgust* (1905) is one such example.

Finally Klee persuaded Lily's disapproving father, a physician, to allow her to marry him. On September 15, 1906, they were married and moved to Munich.

MARRIED LIFE IN MUNICH

Paul and Lily Klee settled into an unconventional domestic routine in a small second-floor apartment in Munich. Lily gave piano lessons and Klee shopped for food, cooked, and cleaned the apartment. When their only child Felix was born on November 30, 1907, Klee took on the responsibility of his care. He painted in the kitchen, while Felix slept. When the weather was good they'd sit on the balcony overlooking the courtyard. Klee would paint what he saw, such as *Street with Carriage* (1907). When Felix was a toddler, they would take walks together with Klee carrying his painting equipment and Felix holding his toys—some of which had been made by Klee himself. He had a treasured sailboat, a puppet theater, even a train that his father had made for him.

It was an idyllic time. In the evenings there was always music. Lily played the piano, Klee, the violin. Friends would arrive and settle in for an evening of music and conversation. There was also much to stimulate the artist in the city of Munich itself. Not only were there concerts but there was a great deal of art. An international city, Munich had many galleries, museums, and exhibitions. In 1908 it was at one of these exhibitions that Klee, at last, saw and admired the French Impressionists, especially the works of Cézanne and van Gogh. When he read the letters of the great Dutch master, he was electrified by his ideals of painting; he was stunned at the artist's expressive, emotive style. He also noted: "His pathos is foreign to me, but he is certainly a genius. . . . This is a brain which is suffering from the burning fire of a star." Klee was even more impressed by Cézanne when he saw eight of his works at a Vienna Secession exhibition in 1908.

Klee's first painting, *Girl with Jugs*, shows Cézanne's influence. Klee was beginning to think strategically about color. He deliberately planned large areas of contrasting color without any shading or blending at their borders. He superimposed these shapes on an actual line drawing, giving the painting depth of tone. The influence of Henri Matisse, too, is evident in the choice of red and blue, and in the painting's contours. But the unsettling expression on the girl's face, her appearance, the carefully thought-out and audacious lines were very much Klee's.

Money was always a problem in Munich. The few works Klee sold and the money he earned from teaching an evening drawing class were not enough to support his household. As he wrote when he turned thirty, "From now on I must be myself." He refused to compromise his art to sell his work.

Klee persevered. One year later, in 1910, he had his first one-man show of fifty-six pieces, exhibited in Bern, Zurich, and Winterthur, Switzerland. His work was well-received in Bern and Zurich; and he sold some pieces. When a woman in Zurich told Klee she was going to actually start collecting his work, he felt confident enough to write to Lily and tell her he could no longer handle all the household chores. He had to devote more time to

18

The Rising of the Moon,
at St. Germain,
Tunis (detail)

painting. Unfortunately, in Winterthur the public hated his work, and the exhibition quickly closed.

But the show gave Klee recognition, not only among the public but also among his colleagues in the art world

THE BLUE RIDERS

Suddenly Klee had a circle of friends, fellow artists and peers who could appreciate and understand him. There was the painter Franz Marc, who became a close friend, and painters Louis Moilliet, Gabriele Münter, August Macke, and Hans Arp, as well as writers and scholars, all of them spending evenings in lengthy discussions of modern art, on its history, and the artists' intent.

One of the most influential of the friendships Klee made during this time was with the Russian painter Wassily Kandinsky. He lived nearby, and Moilliet, who know both Klee and Kandinsky, showed them each other's work. Eventually, in 1911, the two met and a friendship was born, although Kandinsky was much older.

In 1911 Kandinsky founded the Blue Riders (Blaue Reiter), a group of artists who expounded the beliefs of abstract expression- ism, a style that would grow in popularity in the 1940s and 1950s with the work of such American artists as Jackson Pollack and Willem de Kooning. The Blue Riders were influenced by Cubism, but in addition they emphasized the process of painting with vibrant brushstrokes and dramatic color. They tried in their work to reflect their inner impulses and to provoke intense per- sonal reactions from their audiences. They also believed that such sources as children's drawings, oriental paintings, African sculp- ture, and medieval ivories, could be the roots for art's renewal and rebirth.

Kandinsky was a mentor of sorts to Klee and proved to be a great influence, although Klee found his work somewhat "bizarre." Years later, when Klee taught at the Bauhaus, he expounded and refined the views of Kandinsky and the Blue Riders—up to a point. He refuted their theory that art should be separate from the natural world. Like the Cubists, they started with form. To Klee, form was the end result of nature, not the source. Art was an inter- pretation of the natural world in all its aspects. Art sprung from the natural world, created by and evolved by nature and people.

Bahn

Einst dem Grau der Nacht ent taucht / Dan schwer und teuer / und stark vom Feuer /
Abends voll von Gott und gebeugt / Nun ätherlings vom Blau um schauert, / entschwebt
über Firnen, zu klugen Gestirnen.

*After Rising
in the Grayness
of the Night*

Klee wrote that only children, madmen, and primitive people still had, or had rediscovered, the "power to see."

Klee, as always, listened to his own inner song. Contemporary art currents were a source of inspiration, but only up to a point. Cubism was no exception. Cubists, including the Blue Rider group, focused on form; geometric shapes evoked time and space. As Klee wrote in his diary, "Landscape can more easily suffer the proportion of the objects represented to be changed by simplification . . . the result is always a landscape. Animals and men, which are created to live, lose something of their power to live with each deformation."

One notable exception, however, was the French painter Robert Delaunay.

A SECOND TRIP TO PARIS

Klee met Delaunay in the spring of 1912, on a second trip to Paris. Between trips to the opera, to the Latin Quarter, to Montmartre and Notre-Dame, Klee spent some time with the painter. Those few hours would have a tremendous impact on him. In Delaunay's work, he saw that Cubism did not have to be static and that it was possible to create a completely separate and independent picture with its own abstract formality, its own life, its own nature, and its own rules. A painting could be natural and abstract at the same time.

Klee believed Delaunay achieved this goal through light, not in traditional ways. Rather than producing light by increasing or decreasing a single color's tone, Delaunay produced it through movement, through the use of contrasting colors.

Klee admired, in Delaunay's work, the movement that light created. Above all, it was movement that Klee sought in his own art. Movement implied relationships within a composition; it represented depth. Movement created light; it created life.

It was this belief in movement that also drew Klee to Futurism with which he'd come in contact at an exhibition in 1913. Begun four years earlier in Italy, Futurism was reflected in the work of such painters as Marcel Duchamp (*Nude Descending a Staircase*, 1913) and Gino Severini. It glorified movement. But rather than depicting nature, Futurism paid tribute to the modern machine. Rather than creating realistic representations, Futurist artists

Poster for the
Bauhaus Exhibition
of 1923 (detail)

broke forms up into their parts, showing the movements of each simultaneously, abstractly, and multi-dimensionally. Utilizing techniques that made a composition move, that made it dynamic, they tried not only to convey the emotion of the moment, but that of memory and the past, all at the same time.

These theories appealed to Klee. For the next two years, like Delaunay and the Futurists, he used splashes of color and teased surfaces with color, changing composition and boundaries. But he realized he had not yet developed enough. He felt that such paintings as *Mountain Slope* (1914) were too contrived. *Lamp-posts* worked better in that it combined the theories of both the Futurists and Delaunay. But it still wasn't enough. He faced the problem many avant-garde artists of this same period experienced: new concepts, while well-defined on a theoretical level, were not yet producing tangible results.

This would change with Klee's trip to Africa.

TUNISIA

Klee joined his friends Louis Moilliet and August Macke on a seventeen-day trip to Tunisia in 1914. It was an unforgettable experience. Everything about Africa entranced and delighted him. "I am possessed by color—I do not need to pursue it," he wrote. "I know that it will possess me forever. This is the great moment: I and color are one. I am a painter."

For those brief seventeen days, Klee sketched and painted his watercolors, on the streets, in the harbors, while traveling from Tunis to Saint-Germain, from Hammamet to Kairouan. He brought back to Munich the foundations for some of his greatest work.

View of Kairouan is a vivid abstract interpretation, expressing depth of color and line. Both *The Rising of the Moon, at St. Germain, Tunis* and *Motif from Hammamet* have extraordinary spatiality. Here, the influences of Cézanne, Delaunay, and the Futurists combine with Klee's new freedom of color to create a new reality, changing a landscape into an expressive abstract. The colors move into one another without following any rigid geometric borders.

The vivid colors and symbols Klee internalized in Tunisia can also be seen in his later works, in *Sun and Moon* and in *Landscape*

Highways and Byways (detail)

with Yellow Birds (1923). Here is the moon, the palms, the vibrant tones of earth and sky, reveal the constant movement of composition, of life.

Tunisia also reawakened Klee's enthusiasm for Cubism. The small, square Arab houses, the streets, the carpet textures—all this he saw as a celebration of natural form and of lines that "walked" and created their own reality. He took Cubism and created new depth, new realities.

COMING INTO HIS OWN

War broke out in Europe a few months after Klee returned to Munich. Many young artists enlisted. At first Klee appeared relatively indifferent. In 1915 he wrote: "I have had this war within me for some time. For this reason it does not touch the inner me."

As so many Germans believed in the early days of the war, Klee was certain it would be short and Germany would be victorious. Within a year his attitude changed. Supported by the king of Bavaria, a policy exempting the artists of Munich from serving in the army was enforced. Although Klee used the war as a subject for some of his paintings, such as *The Angry Kaiser* (1920), he remained detached.

His paintings continued to sell well and he continued to grow and to somehow make his theories a reality. He was determined, for example, to find a way to combine painting and poetry into one "virtual reality" that through the use of different media would become immediately clear and understood. From the beginning Klee had combined his titles and pictures in a "symbiotic" relationship where one was needed to understand and enhance the other.

But Klee did not fully synthesize written language and art in his compositions until 1916 when Lily gave him a collection of Chinese verse. It proved serendipitous. In the Far East the meaning of a poem is dependent on the position of the words on the page. With these verses Klee now had the solution he needed to combine poetry and painting, exemplified in *After Rising in the Grayness of the Night* (1918). Here is a geometric structure containing smaller squares. Within these squares are letters, clear, luminous, and vividly colored. The letters develop into words, the words into verses (which are believed to be Klee's own poetry) written above the design, making the language one with the composition, the poetry one with the painting, inseparable.

As Klee's theories matured his productivity increased. His paintings became powerful studies of contradiction, pictorial languages all their own. He wanted to make shapes and forms grow into a building, a tree, a moonscape. He became a poet, physicist, architect, and anatomist. Each picture adhered to its own rules, its own language, its own symbols. It is a world of its own and it tells its own truth. Even Klee's materials were unorthodox. He would mix oils with watercolors. He used glue and pumice stones on painted canvas, whatever would bring out the painting's truth, whatever would make "the invisible visible."

In *Myth of the Flower*, for example, Klee combines sexuality, infancy, and flight to create a passionate truth. Here are birds in flight; here are moons and half-moons, trees and dark mysterious borders—all within the confines of a primitive shape that evokes voluptuousness. *Villa R*, one of his most famous paintings, was completed in 1919. It includes the vibrant colors Klee found in Tunisia as well as his fusion of language and form. The walking lines and the powerful symbolic images—such as the cross—evoke a timelessness within the confinement of the finite picture frame.

These and many more paintings, including *The Tree House*, *Arctic Thaw*, *Message of the Air Spirit*, *Rosa*, *Drawings for Plants*, *Soil, and Air*, other oils on larger canvases and on small ones, and drawings and sketches, were proving that Klee was not only a genius but an artist who could continually produce magic. His popularity was growing so fast that the art dealer Hans Goltz drew up a contract with him in which he had sole rights to exhibit his work.

In 1920, Goltz organized a Klee retrospective that included a total of 326. He also arranged the publication of two monographs drawn from Klee's diaries.

Klee was famous.

THE BAUHAUS YEARS

At the end of 1920, Klee was offered a teaching position at the esteemed Bauhaus, the famous school founded in 1919 by the architect Walter Gropius in Weimar, Germany. The school's declared goal was to eliminate the separation between art and crafts, between the artist and artisan, and to create a unity between function and design. To that end Gropius invited some of most

27

*Struck Off
the List*

famous architects, designers, and artists to teach at the school and promote the ideas of structure and function as art. The architect Mies van der Rohe joined him, as did the abstract artists Laszlo Moholy-Nagy and Lyonel Feininger. Kandinsky came from Moscow with his young wife, as did many other painters from the Blue Rider group. The Bauhaus, which today is synonymous with clean, functional design, also had as its ideal a unity of all the arts. Here artists were craftsmen, albeit superior ones, devoted to this common goal. And in 1921 the name Paul Klee was added to the roster of esteemed artists and architects.

It was a unique experience for Klee. For the first time he had a guaranteed income and security. During his five-year association with the Bauhaus Klee was free to explore his theories of composition, structure, and the function of art. "Pictures look at us," he told his students. Later he added: "The artist contemplates what nature sets before his eyes. . . . And the more deeply he penetrates, the easier it is for him to shift the viewpoint from today to yesterday, the more will be impressed on his mind . . . the one essential image, that of creation as genesis." Klee compared the creation of the world with the creation of a work of art, a dynamic, natural process that gives birth to form—and life.

Some of Klee's most famous paintings were completed at Weimar. *The Twittering Machine* (1922) has a delicate and precise chromatic layout. It is incisive and expressive, a comment on faith in the mechanical age. The birds, so often a symbol in Klee's work, are a contraption making "bird song." The painting, done in pen and watercolor, gently mocks people's undivided belief in machines and their purely sentimental love of bird song. *Fish Magic* (1925) is an underwater dreamscape. Here fish, flowers, and even people as visitors demonstrate that anything is possible in the world of dreams.

God of the Northern Forest (1922) is another masterpiece from Klee's Bauhaus years. This is a dark work with flowing violets, greens, and yellows. In the midst of this color is an almost indistinguishable face composed of geometric forms.

The Gold Fish, completed in 1925, utilizing oil and watercolor on paper, is an astonishing study of color. The golden warmth of the fish glows undimmed by the deep blue of the surrounding sea. The power of *The Gold Fish* has given rise to many interpretations.

The most popular is that the painting symbolizes a love that cannot be extinguished.

During the Bauhaus years Klee also produced his magic squares. These paintings, composed of rhythmic chromatic relationships, are a brilliant contrast between a mathematical grid structure and the rich density and resonance of color pigments. These magic squares include *Table of Color in Gray Major* and *Blossoming.*

In 1929, Klee finished *Highways and Byways,* one of his most famous paintings. Here, the inclination of the lines suggests a landscape. Their movement suggests fast movement, an abstraction and an essence of highway movement.

While at the Bauhaus Klee enjoyed a soaring fame. In 1929, to coincide with his fiftieth birthday, a large commemorative exhibition opened in Berlin. Simultaneously, the gallery owner Flechtheim presented 150 of Klee's works.

But as the years passed Klee became more and more absorbed in his own intense research, in his attempt to combine the abstract and the personal, his roles of mystic and mathematician, intellectual and poet. His teaching began to encroach more and more upon his art. At first, he simply reduced the number of classes he taught. Unfortunately, that activated academic politics as colleagues and administrators disagreed over his absences. Added to this was right-wing pressure to close the school. In 1931, a few months before the Bauhaus ceased to exist, Klee left.

DÜSSELDORF AND BEYOND

The Academy in Düsseldorf was far from the excitement of the Bauhaus. But the lectures in painting and drawing Klee gave as a teacher enabled him to work unrestrained on his own.

Klee was always "reinventing" himself, experimenting with new techniques, styles, and colors to get closer to his version of truth, where the world is one. Thus, his paintings and drawings at different times in his development are vastly different from one another. *Ad Parnassum*, painted while Klee was at Düsseldorf, is one of his most encompassing works, a synthesis of various techniques and principles. There are echoes of pointillism here (tiny dot-like brushstrokes to create form), which Klee called Divisionism. Cubism and expressive abstraction are represented, and even Impressionistic painting is suggested in its deep sense of color. *Ad*

Parnassum has a mathematical construction. The dense grids covering the composition suggest a mosaic. The pervasive sense of peace in the painting, its spiritual subject, suggests that at this time Klee was not encumbered with economic worries and overdemanding teaching schedules and was a painter at the height of his power, serene in the work he was creating.

Unfortunately, this peace lasted only three years. By 1933 the Nazis had come to power in Germany. They required all employees of the state to demonstrate their Aryan origins. Failure to do so would result in immediate dismissal. Although Klee abhorred the law, he wanted to paint, and he decided to obtain the documents he needed to prove his non-Jewish origins. The rules, however, changed in midstream. Not only did he have to prove his origins, he had to declare his loyalty to the Nazi regime. Klee refused to do so. He was dismissed from the Academy on April 21, 1933.

This dismissal spurred Klee's productivity. In 1933 alone he created 482 works of art, including the powerful *Struck Off the List*, a profound self-portrait that reflects a terrible anger and sadness. The large X covering part of the forehead and cheek seems to echo, underline, and perpetuate Klee's feelings.

The difficult period had begun.

THE END OF THE CYCLE

Klee moved back to Bern, but it was a return fraught with isolation and alienation. Switzerland lacked the creative stimuli he had become accustomed to in Germany. In addition, his finances started to strain and his economic situation was once again precarious. Even worse, his popularity had began to diminish. The exhibition in the Kunsthalle of Bern in 1935 did not draw as many collectors as he had hoped.

Then, at the end of 1935, Klee came down with the symptoms of progressive scleroderma, the disease that would eventually kill him.

The year 1936 was a difficult one for Klee. He was in too much pain to do more than twenty-five pieces. But from 1937 to 1939 his output increased in an instinctive rush against time. His style changed. His paintings became bigger and bolder. They had black borders and he used thick paint. His subjects became symbols that were often ambiguous. Many of these paintings reflect death and the Nazi regime but they also have great vitality and energy.

Revolution of the Viaduct (1937) is one of Klee's most famous works and is unanimously considered a painting inspired by the profound historical and political destruction surrounding him. The arches, as they seem to march toward the observer, can be considered a challenge to Nazism; they trample something, perhaps the uniformity of the restraining and repressive order. Indeed, as Klee finished *Revolution*, the Nazis were organizing, in Munich, a "degenerate art" exhibit, in which a number of Klee's works were included. The catalogue defined them as "the work of a sick mind."

Other works in these final years include the highly abstract *Park Near Lu* (Lucerne), painted in 1938, which captures the feeling of space and movement, of landscape, and of the noise and emotions of the park visitors within its frame. *Insula Dulcamara* is one of the largest pictures Klee ever painted. Here within this "fabulous island" is a face with dark eye sockets that could represent death, as does the *Angels* series, *Eidola*, and the *Passion*. In these paintings Klee seems determined to go further inward—toward the essence of life and "to the heart of creation."

Klee's illness became worse in 1940. He went to the hospital at Locarno, Switzerland, where he died on June 29, 1940, just days before he was to be granted a Swiss citizenship. On an easel in his apartment stood his last painting. *Still Life* contained a jug, some vases, and flowers on a table. They are dense with color. The background is black. An angel carries a cross off in the corner. There is no signature.

"I belong not only to this life. I live well with the dead, as with those not born. Nearer to the heart of creation than others. But still too far."

These words were inscribed on Klee's tombstone by his son Felix. They exemplify his lifelong struggle to combine dichotomies, contrasts, and opposites, because in that combination, in that perfect moment of inner and outer vision, creation begins.

32

Sentimental Virgin with Daisy

Garden Scene with Watering Cans

Garden Still Life with Watering Can

Klee

Motif aus Hammamet 1914 48

Motif from Hammamet

1915 102

South Wind in Marc's Garden

1916 . 19.

Miniature

1916. 70.

The Fish in the Harbor

City of Churches

Flower Myth

Still Life with Thistle

Garden

The Lamb

The Lamb (detail)

Growth of Nocturnal Plants

1921/69 Fug

Fugue in Red

Young Girl's Adventure

Still Life with Snake

Klee

1942 / 30

Wandbild aus dem Tempel der Sehnsucht "dorthin"

Mural from the Temple of Yearning ↖Thither ↗

Senecio

Senecio (detail)

1923 134 Rot

Rotation

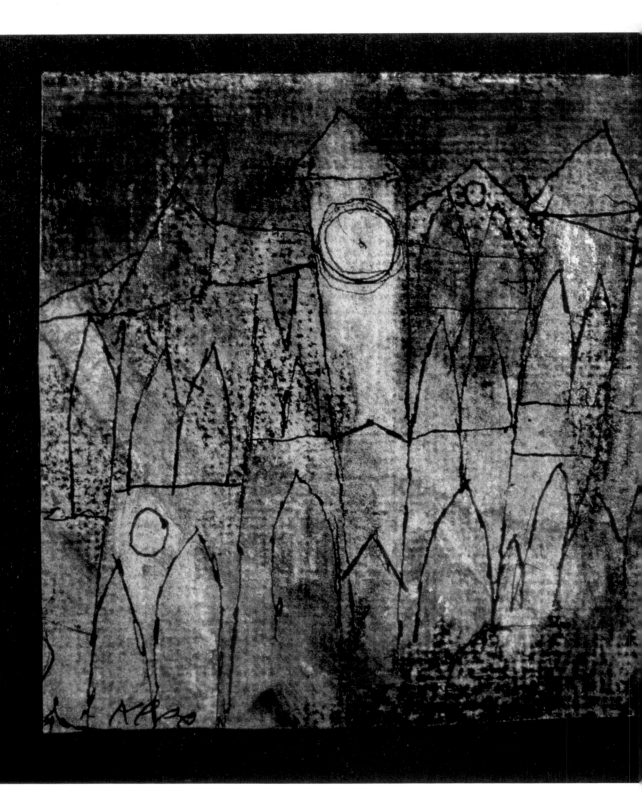

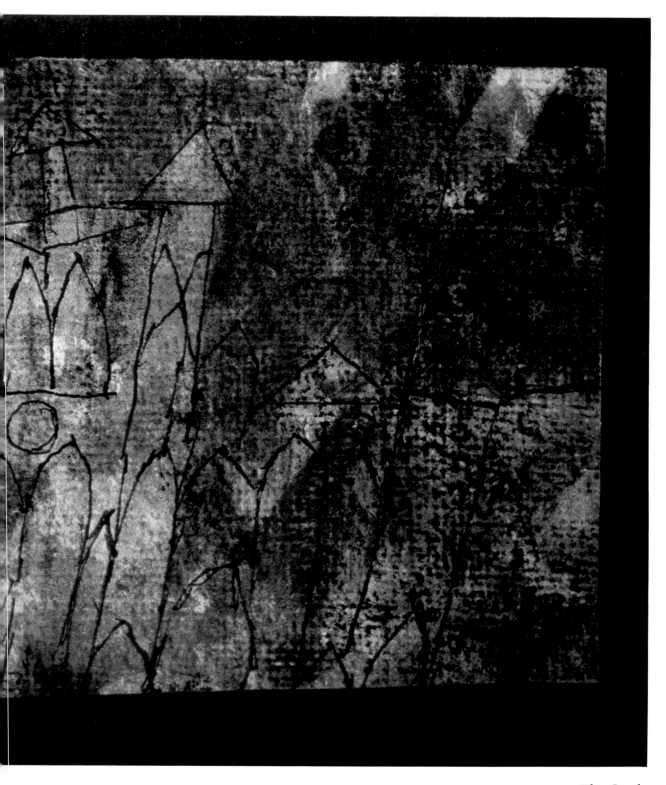

The Castle

Dwarf (Fairy Tale)

Dwarf (Fairy Tale) (detail)

The Gold Fish

1925. 1. Flo

Flotilla

Stage Rehearsal

1927 Y5. Partie aus G.

View of G

Sun and Moon

Sun and Moon (detail)

III

1930 H. 2. nach

lhende Landschaft

Untitled

Untitled (detail)

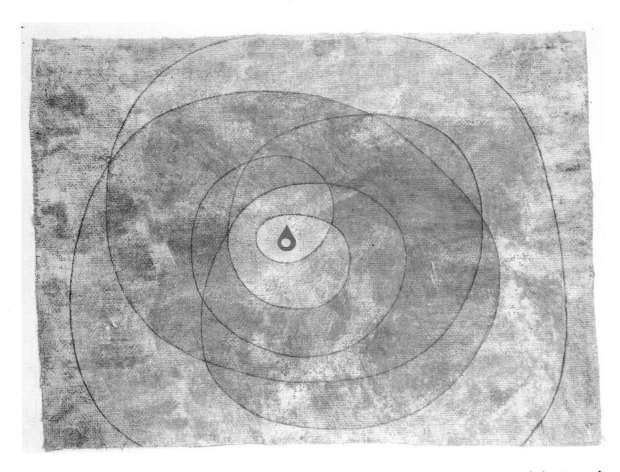

Around the Kernel

Mystic Ceramic

Still Life with Casket

Cathedral

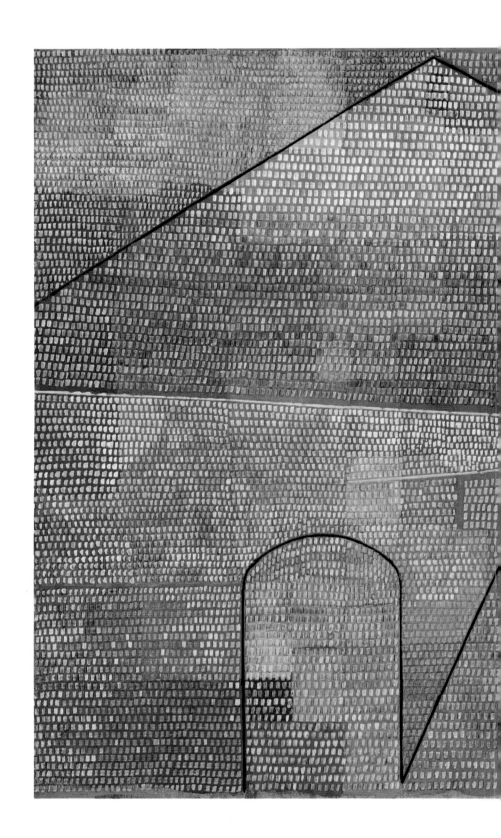

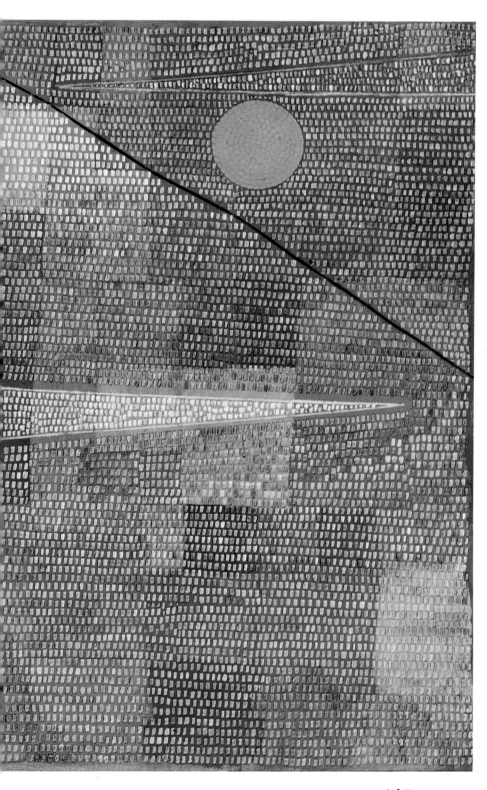

Ad Parnassum

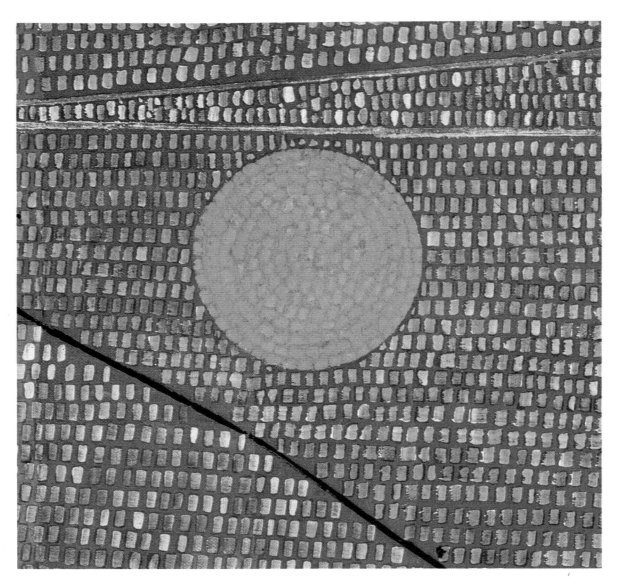

Ad Parnassum (detail)

Park Near Lu(cerne)

Insula Dulcamara

Insula Dulcamara (detail)

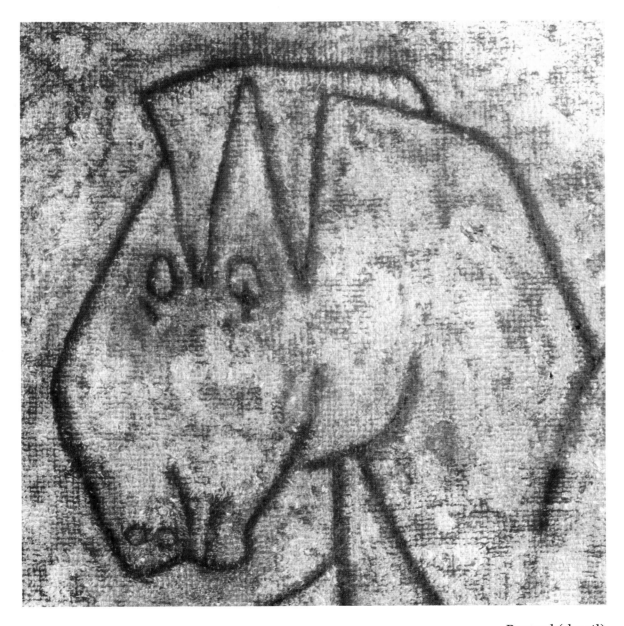

Bastard (detail)

Bastard

Flowers in Stone